DIGITAL AND INFORMATION LITERACY ™

CITED!

IDENTIFYING CREDIBLE INFORMATION ONLINE

LARRY GERBER

rosen publishing's
rosen central

NEW YORK

For Lisa and Matt

Published in 2011 by The Rosen Publishing Group, Inc.
29 East 21st Street, New York, NY 10010

Library of Congress Cataloging-in-Publication Data

Gerber, Larry, 1946–
Cited! identifying credible information online / Larry Gerber. — 1st ed.
    p. cm. — (Digital and information literacy)
Includes bibliographical references and index.
ISBN 978-1-4358-9430-3 (library binding)
ISBN 978-1-4488-0599-0 (pbk)
ISBN 978-1-4488-0600-3 (6-pack)
1. Internet research—Juvenile literature. 2. Electronic information resource literacy—Juvenile literature. 3. Computer network resources—Evaluation—Juvenile literature. I. Title.
ZA4228.G47 2010
001.4'202854678—dc22

2010003050

Manufactured in the United States of America

CPSIA Compliance Information: Batch #CG115130YA: For further information, contact Rosen Publishing, New York, New York, at 1-800-237-9932.

CONTENTS

INTRODUCTION

It's hard to imagine doing research without the Internet. Just fifteen years ago, finding the simplest information could take a long time. Conducting research usually involved a trip to the library to search for the right books and papers. Librarians could help people find books, but to find facts, researchers had to turn lots of pages and do a lot of reading.

Finding audio or video information could take even longer. A researcher had to listen to the radio or watch television until useful material came on, record it, and then transcribe it so it could be used later. Digging up a photograph was often an impossible task.

In the days before digital pictures and sound, companies, schools, and governments hired dozens of people to search and keep track of words, pictures, and tapes. Today, all it takes is an Internet connection and a computer. A middle school student with a laptop can gather more information in an hour than any predigital expert could. That's great news, but it creates a whole new set of problems. While it's easy to get information from the Internet, it's also easy for anyone to put information out there. And information does not equal fact.

Much of the information on the Internet is someone's opinion. Opinions—people's beliefs, likes, and dislikes—can't be tested and proved. Opinions are not facts.

Online information can also be incorrect. Sometimes a source of information can make an honest mistake. But not everyone is honest. Sometimes sources deliberately publish incorrect information. A big part of research is checking information to see whether it's correct or not—whether it's actually a fact.

Even when solid facts are identified, they aren't always useful. Facts may be out of date. Or maybe they simply don't apply to the subject being researched. Another important part of research is determining which facts are relevant and which ones are not. After checking facts to make sure they're correct and useful, it's important to be sure they are being used in the right way.

Researchers need to build a foundation of facts in order to reach solid conclusions. This book is about finding facts in a jumble of information. It's also about choosing facts that are relevant to a research topic, and presenting those facts in a way that's fair to the source and helpful to the people who will someday use the research.

Chapter 1

Facts and Where to Find Them

Facts are information that we know is true. Facts can be proved or confirmed. Researchers often use media to find facts, which originate with sources. What exactly are media, and what are sources?

Media is the plural of the word "medium." Information media carry words, sound, and pictures from sources to users. Media includes books, magazines, movies, newspapers, radio, telephones, television, and even handwritten notes. The Internet can be used to access all those media, so the Internet is a kind of super-medium.

Sources are the starting points of information. Sources are usually people or groups of people. When a friend phones to say that a study group meets at 8 , the medium is the phone; the source is the friend. If a student checks http://www.census.gov to find out what the current U.S. population is, the medium is the Internet; the source is the U.S. Census Bureau.

The most important quality of a source is credibility. When a source is credible, it means that the source's information can be believed. To judge credibility, it's important to be clear about the difference between sources

Before the Internet, a researcher might have spent hours looking for information in the library. Computers often make research easier, but books are still important information sources.

and media. If someone asks where a piece of information comes from, he or she is asking for the source. Saying "I saw it on television" doesn't answer the question. Television is a medium, not a source.

This distinction is important because the Internet can be used to tap into a wide variety of media to find sources. It helps to keep in mind the difference between Web pages and other material found on the Web. Web pages are designed and written specifically for Internet users. But the Internet can also be used to access pages of magazines, newspapers, books, and video and audio files. Credible sources in all media usually reveal their sources of information so they can be checked for accuracy.

File   Edit   View   Favorites   Tools   Help

CREDIBLE WEB PAGES

Credible Web Pages

Here's an example of the difference between a Web page and other types of media material that can be found on the Web.

A Google search for "causes of wars" will probably yield a Wikipedia page as its top result. Who wrote the article? It doesn't say. Sources are cited for some of the information, but other sections don't say where the information came from.

A search for "causes of wars" using Google Scholar yields different results, however. Instead of Wikipedia and other Web pages, the search returns a list of books and papers. Most have been reviewed by experts, fact-checked, and edited. The authors' names are usually right at the top, and the authors cite sources for the facts they use. In addition, the pages turned up by Google Scholar contain information that has been published in places other than the Web. Which seems to be the most credible: the Wikipedia page or the pages returned by Google Scholar?

Primary and Secondary Sources

There are two main types of sources: primary and secondary. Primary sources provide firsthand information. For example, people involved in an accident are primary sources of information about the accident. So are people who saw the accident. Primary sources are often in the best position to know what happened.

Autobiographies, or books written by people about themselves, are primary sources, as are people's diaries. Experts can be primary sources

People who have seen or experienced something firsthand are primary sources of information about that subject. Interviewers, who get information from primary sources, are secondary sources.

about a specific topic: People like doctors and scientists who have studied something for years can provide firsthand information about it. Some primary sources aren't people. Photos, paintings, coins, statues, pottery, and other artifacts can tell researchers a lot about the times when they were created.

Secondary sources take their facts from primary sources. Secondary sources include reference books, articles, nonfiction books, and television programs. They also include biographies, or books written about people by others. Secondary sources give the benefit of analysis and perspective.

Journalists are common secondary sources. Reporters don't always witness the events that they report, but they usually talk to people who did. People who report news for a living are often credible because they have been trained for their jobs and their livelihood depends on their credibility. Most of their reporting can be checked for accuracy against other news stories. Print reporting usually has more detail than reporting on radio and television.

The Internet has made new kinds of reporting possible. Today, many reputable journalists and news organizations maintain blogs and Twitter accounts. However, a number of people who haven't been trained as journalists also keep blogs and write articles. Some pass along their comments on Twitter or other social media. These people are sometimes known as citizen journalists. There are millions of potential citizen journalists, and they are often in places where there are no regular journalists. They may find information that regular journalists don't have.

The fact that a citizen journalist may have been the only person to witness an event makes it hard to check his or her information. Sometimes it's impossible to know the true identity of bloggers and those who use Twitter, so it's usually best to be careful about using such sources. It is impossible to judge whether or not a source is credible if nothing is known about the source.

One of the first things that we need to determine about a source is whether he or she is qualified to give us accurate information. In other words, we need to determine if the source is in a position to know the facts.

Recognizing Bias

"Bias" is a term that describes a slanted or prejudiced point of view. Everyone has a point of view, and everyone presents information from that viewpoint. No one, not even the best source, can be entirely free of bias. We all have our points of view and our likes and dislikes. Professional reporters are taught to watch out for their personal biases and keep them out of their reporting as much as possible.

Professional journalists are taught to avoid personal bias, but everyone has a unique viewpoint. Newspeople often report things in different ways because they have different ideas of what's important.

However, some bias is intentional. Some sources want others to see things as they do and therefore intentionally leave out important facts. They may also treat trivial facts as being important. Biased sources usually don't reveal why they want to slant the information.

When we suspect bias, we should ask ourselves these questions:

- Is my source emphasizing some facts and downplaying others?
- If so, why?
- How could the source benefit by slanting the information?

The best way to detect bias is to check the source against other sources. In fact, it's often the only way. That's why researchers try to have at least two sources for every piece of information. When it comes to sources, more is always better.

Using multiple sources to test for credibility is a two-step process. The first step is to find out what others say about the source. Is he or she a Nobel Prize scholar? A veteran reporter? A notorious practical joker? If the source is credible, proceed to the second step, which is to find out if other sources agree with the information. Do other sources say something slightly different? Do they say something entirely different? For most topics, there are plenty of sources available on the Internet or in the library. With practice, bias becomes easier to spot.

Chapter 2

Phony Facts

Knowing what bad information looks like can help researchers avoid it. Let's look at four of the most common ways that sources give us biased or incorrect information. The main problem areas are: opinion disguised as fact, propaganda, misinformation, and disinformation.

Opinion Disguised as Fact

Facts are the basis of research because they can be tested to determine whether they are true or false. Research isn't based on opinion, as opinions are never true or false. If we can prove something, it isn't an opinion. It's a fact. Researchers need to be on the lookout for opinion disguised as fact.

Everybody's entitled to an opinion. But credible sources clearly indicate when they're giving their opinion. Reliable newspapers, for example, put opinion columns and letters on their editorial pages, not their news pages.

Unreliable sources are so sure about their opinion that they really believe it's fact. And some sources don't know the difference.

On their Comedy Central shows, comedians Stephen Colbert *(left)* and Jon Stewart *(right)* get many of their laughs by mocking what they see as bias in reporting by the major news organizations.

When confused about the difference between fact and opinion, a good test is to look at where a source got his or her information. Sources who state facts should have no trouble saying where they got the information. Look out for phrases like "Everybody knows . . ." and "It's obvious that . . ." Those are signals that the next phrase might be an opinion disguised as a fact.

Propaganda

Propaganda is information that promotes a certain point of view. Propaganda isn't always false, but it's always biased.

Most credible newspapers put nothing but news on their front pages. When the *Los Angeles Times* put a paid advertisement on page one, many of its reporters got angry at the paper's owners.

Much of the propaganda that we see is found in advertising. People selling products or services understandably present them in the best possible light. Advertising is everywhere in media. Newspapers, magazines, and broadcast programs all earn money by advertising. Many blogs do as well. Credible media sources keep their advertising and their factual information clearly separate.

A lot of propaganda is political. People looking to get support for their cause or get people to vote for them often make biased statements to promote their ideas. Before accepting "facts" from a politician or political party, it helps to compare them with an opposing view.

Propaganda is often used as a political tool. These propaganda posters in the North Korean capital of Pyongyang were designed to glorify Communist rule.

Personal propaganda has flourished with the Internet. People publish their information and comments on the Web for lots of reasons—anything from finding a job to getting a date. Most people want to look good, so their information is often biased. And it's often hard to check.

Social propaganda promotes all sorts of causes. For instance, groups that want to protect endangered turtles, raise money for hungry children, or end war might use propaganda to promote their cause. Even if a cause is worthy, it's unlikely that these sources will present information that hurts their efforts.

Propaganda may contain facts that are accurate and fair to use in research. However, propaganda seldom shows the whole picture and usually provides only one side of an argument. Good researchers find opposing points of view for balance.

One way to detect propaganda is to ask: Why is the source presenting this information? People who publish propaganda have a reason for going to all the trouble of doing so. Knowing the reason why a source is publishing propaganda can help sort out the facts from the fiction.

Misinformation and Disinformation

Everybody makes mistakes, even sources with the best of intentions. Honest mistakes are known as misinformation. People can be wrong, or misinformed, and still believe they're perfectly correct. This is because memory isn't always reliable and we all tend to see things in different ways.

For instance, people sometimes write their autobiographies years after the events they describe occurred. Historians treat such accounts with great care because they know that people's memories can be unreliable.

When sources make mistakes on purpose, it is disinformation. And it's not always bad. Some Web sites publish hilarious news satires. People use Photoshop to alter pictures for the same kind of laughs. Disinformation can be funny as long as we know it isn't real.

_ ☐ X

File   Edit   View   Favorites   Tools   Help

A SIMPLE TEST

A Simple Test

Sometimes it's possible to spot phony facts just by looking at them. When there is doubt about a source's accuracy, conducting this simple two-part test may help:

1. Do a Web search using the source's name. What do others say about the source? What are the source's qualifications? What does the source do for a living? Does the source have anything to gain by slanting the information?
2. Find material similar to that of the source by doing a search using key phrases from the source's material. Does this material agree with the source's material? Has anybody else used the source's material?

If the source fails either part of the test, don't trust it. Dump the source and move on. Check the comparison material from the second step for possible new sources.

But disinformation can also be used for evil. Dictators like Adolf Hitler and Joseph Stalin commanded huge propaganda organizations that doctored pictures and spread lies about political enemies and minorities. Millions died because people believed the vicious disinformation spread by these regimes. Governments are especially tempted to spread disinformation during wartime. They may compare their enemies to animals or accuse them of atrocities in order to make their own populations more willing to fight.

Rumor and gossip are two other types of disinformation. Unethical media use rumor and gossip to attract readers and advertisers. There are also people who simply don't know what the truth is and don't care. They will put bad information on the Web just because they can.

Warning Signs: Tips for Spotting the Phonies

How can phony "facts" be distinguished from real ones? Remember to ask: Who says? Reliable sources give attribution for things they say—they make it a point to let us know where the information came from so that we can check it for ourselves. Attribution is a source's way of saying, "I didn't make this up." If there's no attribution in the source material, treat it with suspicion.

Exaggeration and innuendo are also things to look out for. Another word for exaggeration is "hyperbole," or "hype." Some news organizations hype stories and facts to make them seem more important than they really are. "Innuendo" is a word that means saying something without really putting it into words, or saying something indirectly. We see examples in news stories that ask questions without answering them—for instance, an article that shows a picture of a man's face with the headline: "Is This Man a Murderer?" If it has been proved that the man is a murderer, the headline should say so. Otherwise, it shouldn't be implied.

Mistakes in writing and punctuation can be another sign of source trouble. Everybody makes mistakes, but if a source is careless with spelling and grammar, we have to wonder how careful the source is with facts.

Emotional and inflammatory language is a strong indicator of bias. Racial slurs and hate speech are extreme examples of this. Other kinds of emotional language appeal to our pity, envy, pride, or other feelings, rather than our thinking. Emotional language can be deceiving. For instance, a charity that helps sick children might use very emotional language to appeal for donations. Although the organization might seem credible and the cause worthy (who wouldn't want to help sick kids?), it's best to take a closer look. Does the organization say that it has actually helped any children? Does the organization have any proof of its success?

Chapter 3

Do the Facts Fit the Subject?

There are a number of ways to tell if information is accurate. After thinking about the question, "Is this information true?," it's time to ask, "Does this information matter?"

Information is posted on the Internet every minute, but not all of it is new. By searching online, we can find pictures and writing that is hundreds of years old. Depending on the subject of our research, the age of our information can make a big difference.

For example, a person writing about social networks on the Web might land on a page that claims Facebook and MySpace get about the same number of visitors. After checking, it turns out that the page is a reliable source. This being the case, it would appear that the information is reliable, too. Or is it? A closer look reveals that the page was posted in June 2008. Since that time, Facebook has become much more popular than MySpace and receives many more visitors.

Subjects that people read about, talk about, and write about every day are known as topical subjects. They include anything that's in the news and just about anything to do with the Internet.

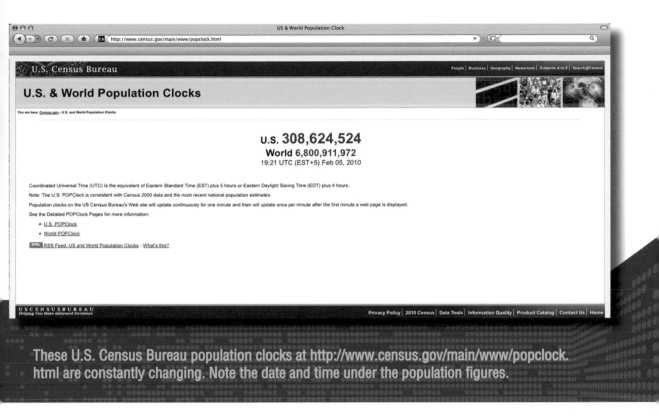

These U.S. Census Bureau population clocks at http://www.census.gov/main/www/popclock.html are constantly changing. Note the date and time under the population figures.

When researching a topical subject, it's important to get the most recent information. It's also a good idea to include the date of the information in research papers.

Some subjects aren't time-sensitive. Good material on subjects like history, math, and some fields of science was written years ago. Historians and scientists are constantly doing new work, and good researchers are always checking to see what's new. But basic facts about subjects like the life of Julius Caesar or how humans digest food don't change in important ways every day.

Does It Really Matter?

Practically all news in the United States comes to us through commercial media. Commercial media is controlled by corporations that sell advertising in order to stay in business. Having a lot of readers and viewers allows a corporation to charge more money for advertising. As a result, it's natural for newspapers, Web sites, television news programs, and radio stations to make their news seem important.

One way to make information seem more important is to present it in a way that touches an emotion. This practice is known as sensationalism. For instance, news of murders and kidnappings gets people's attention. By reading the headlines and experiencing the emotions that they arouse, a person might think that crime is getting out of hand. However, the fact is that the U.S. Justice Department says violent crime has been declining for the past twenty-five years. The reporting on each individual crime may be perfectly accurate, but sensationalism can give the false idea that crime is on the rise.

Glamour and celebrities are also used to get attention and sell ads. Cool pictures are fun to look at, and cool people are fun to read about. However, celebrity and trendiness are often just forms of sensationalism. Just because something is new and cool doesn't mean that it's important.

File   Edit   View   Favorites   Tools   Help

SERIOUS INFORMATION?

Serious Information?

Sometimes the look of a Web page provides clues about the quality of information that it has. Weird wallpaper? Lots of different fonts in different colors? Cute icons? Quirky little apps? These can be warning signs. If a site doesn't have a serious design, it might be good to consider whether or not it contains serious information.

There's nothing wrong with interesting graphic elements. And facts don't have to look dull. However, it's more important that the page be functional. Does the site have useful information? Do all the site's links work? Do the links connect to credible sources? Do the links connect to information about the site?

The format of a medium does not necessarily mean that its information is relevant, either. Many Web pages, newspaper and magazine pages, TV shows, and radio programs have a specific format. This means that they always use the same logos, typefaces, theme music, or studio sets. Radio and TV announcers often say the same thing at the beginning and end of each program. Formatting is a way of making the presentation familiar. Things that feel familiar naturally seem more credible, whether or not they really are.

Jargon

All kinds of experts and specialists, from scientists to ballplayers, have special ways of speaking. People who write reports for businesses, schools, and governments are notorious for using lots of big words in long sentences. This sort of language is known as jargon.

Jargon helps specialists communicate among themselves, but it's not always a good way to communicate with others. Such material often sounds official and important, like something that might be necessary to pay attention to in the course of research.

Sometimes people really do need complicated language to convey an important idea. Researchers may have to go to the dictionary time and again to sort out a tough passage. However, just because it sounds important doesn't mean that it is. Big words can be a cover for dinky ideas. Some people use jargon just because it makes them sound like experts. When good writers need to communicate something important, they try to put it in language that everybody can understand.

Graphs and charts are a great way to show us complicated information. But just as language should be clear, so should graphics. And they need to be relevant. People who write long reports are sometimes tempted to throw in graphics just to break up pages of print. Graphics can be used as filler to pad out an article or make reports look more "factual" without adding much information.

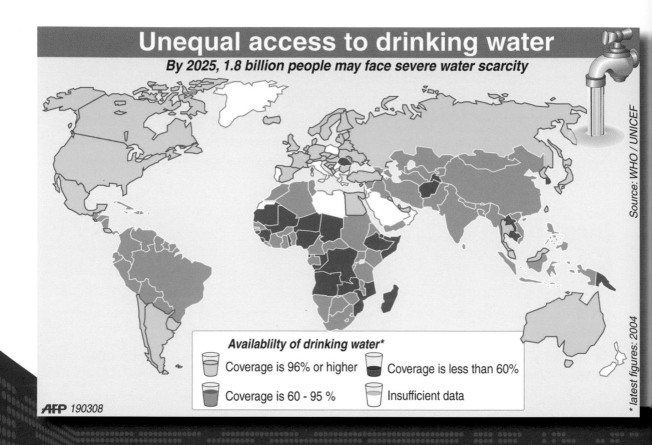

Unequal access to drinking water
By 2025, 1.8 billion people may face severe water scarcity

Availablilty of drinking water*

Coverage is 96% or higher

Coverage is less than 60%

Coverage is 60 - 95 %

Insufficient data

Source: WHO / UNICEF

* latest figures: 2004

AFP 190308

Graphics can show readers a lot of complicated information in a way that's easy to understand, as long as the graphics are clear and relevant to the topic.

Medium vs. Message

There are many ways that researchers can be misled by irrelevant material. Some experts believe we can be influenced not only by the information we get through the media but also by the media themselves.

That's because we use different parts of our brains to process the information we read, hear, and see on a screen or in photos. Media theories can be complicated and controversial, but it's helpful to know some of the basic ideas.

the WHITE HOUSE *PRESIDENT BARACK OBAMA* ★ ★ ★ ★ THE WHITE HOUSE *WASHINGTON* ★ ★ ★   Get Email Updates | Contact Us

BLOG   **PHOTOS & VIDEO**   **BRIEFING ROOM**   **ISSUES**   *the* **ADMINISTRATION**   *the* **WHITE HOUSE**   *our* **GOVERNMENT**

Home • *The White House Blog*

Search WhiteHouse.gov   Search

The White House Blog

Subscribe

President Barack Obama's Inaugural Address

Posted by **Macon Phillips** on January 21, 2009 at 01:27 PM EST

Yesterday, President Obama delivered his Inaugural Address, calling for a "new era of responsibility." Watch the video here:

(download .mp4)

00:00 / 21:22

Inaugural Address

By President Barack Hussein Obama

My fellow citizens: I stand here today humbled by the task before us, grateful for the trust you've bestowed, mindful of the sacrifices borne by our ancestors.

I thank President Bush for his service to our nation -- (applause) -- as well as the generosity and cooperation he has shown throughout this transition.

Forty-four Americans have now taken the presidential oath. The words have been spoken during rising tides of prosperity and the still waters of peace. Yet, every so often, the oath is taken amidst gathering clouds and raging storms. At these moments, America has carried on not simply because of the skill or vision of those in high office, but because we, the people, have remained faithful to the ideals of our forebears and true to our founding documents.

So it has been; so it must be with this generation of Americans.

That we are in the midst of crisis is now well understood. Our nation is at war against a far-reaching network of

WHITE HOUSE BLOGS

The White House Blog

Middle Class Task Force Blog

Council on Environmental Quality

Office of Management and Budget Blog

Office of Public Engagement

Office of Science & Tech Policy Blog

Open Government Blog

Partnerships Blog

US Trade Representative Blog

HELP *for* HAITI

Learn What You Can Do

CATEGORIES

Civil Rights
Defense
Disabilities
Economy
Education
Energy & Environment
Ethics
Family
Fiscal Responsibility
Foreign Policy
Health Care
Homeland Security
Immigration
Poverty
Rural

This page on the White House Blog (http://www.whitehouse.gov/blog) is a good example of multimedia on the Web. It lets us see a speech, hear it, and read it. We use different parts of our brains for those three jobs.

Let's say that one person watches a speech on television. Another hears it on the radio, and another reads it on a Web site. Each person is likely to have different ideas about the speech and about what parts of it were important.

On television, the speaker may smile and gesture. Viewers will be influenced just by the way that he or she looks. A radio audience won't be influenced by how the speaker looks, but they will be influenced by the speaker's pauses and tone of voice.

Do those things matter for a person's research? They might, if the person's topic is the speaker. If the reader is concerned only about the speaker's information, it's a good idea for him or her to actually read the speech.

Getting material in writing not only helps eliminate mistakes, but it also helps a researcher judge the importance of the material—as opposed to the way the material is presented.

Chapter 4

Rules and Fair Play

We have looked at ways to make sure that our source material is accurate and that it's relevant. After accumulating accurate and relevant source material, there is another question to think about before putting the information in a research paper: is it being used fairly?

Plagiarism

Plagiarism means taking somebody else's words or ideas and passing them off as one's own without giving credit to the source. Plagiarism is a type of theft.

Professional researchers and respected writers, some with advanced degrees and years of experience, have lost their jobs and reputations because of plagiarism. Sometimes they lose money, too. Courts can impose fines for violations of copyright law, which protects much written material, works of art, music, and computer programs.

For students, plagiarism results in failing grades. In some cases, people are kicked out of school.

Research isn't just copying information. It also means keeping track of information sources so the sources can be credited.

Getting caught is easier than it might seem. Several Web sites offer search engines designed for teachers to check for plagiarized material. Tracking down stolen research is pretty simple, even without a special search engine.

The main victims of plagiarism are the ones who commit it. A big part of research is learning things for ourselves and learning how to communicate what we've learned. The process of learning and communicating gets more complicated in high school and college.

- □ X

File   Edit   View   Favorites   Tools   Help

SAVING SOURCE INFORMATION

Saving Source Information

The computer's copy-and-paste function is a great way to save source material. It's also ideal to save attribution material at the same time. Professional researchers usually keep the following items so that they can use them when it's time to cite their sources:

- The name of the source.
- The name of the media carrying the information: titles of books, magazines, newspapers, radio or TV programs, and Web sites.
- Web addresses for Internet material.
- The date the material was published or posted.
- The date it was accessed, if it came from an Internet source. This can be important because Web pages sometimes disappear.

Student researchers don't always have to provide all these items in their research papers, but they can come in handy if they are kept on file.

People become better at things by practicing. Athletes and musicians have to do a great deal of practicing if they hope to improve. A student who claims to have practiced when he or she really didn't may manage to get a good grade or credit. However, the student won't get any better at sports or music. So what's going to happen when it's time to play in front of an audience?

Research isn't as difficult or complicated as it's often made out to be. Most researchers, especially students, are expected to use the work of others. But they're expected to use it fairly and correctly. It's easy to avoid plagiarism.

The key to doing so is to use proper attribution. Attribution is the process of naming one's sources of information and giving credit where it's due.

When to Attribute

Some assignments require attribution in footnotes or endnotes, particularly for college-level work and beyond. Instructors will usually say what format to use and how much information should be given. Certain types of information should always be attributed to a source. They are:

- Direct quotations
- Paraphrasing
- Ideas that are taken from a source
- Statistics and other data provided by a source

Let's look at how each one might appear in a research paper.

Quotations

Quotations are a source's exact words. They should always go inside quotation marks, and the source should be cited directly before or after the quotation. The following example, which includes a made-up quotation from a made-up source, shows the proper way to format a quotation:

> "The studies that we have conducted over the past ten years show that drivers between the ages of sixteen and nineteen react more quickly than drivers over fifty years of age," says Dr. Michelle Richards of the National Auto Safety Administration.

Paraphrases

Paraphrases are similar to quotations, but they don't use the source's exact words. People often paraphrase to shorten direct quotations or make them clearer. Paraphrases don't go inside quotation marks. The source should be cited directly before or after the paraphrase:

> Studies over the past ten years show that teenage drivers have quicker reactions than drivers over fifty, according to Dr. Michelle Richards of the National Auto Safety Administration.

Ideas

We should attribute ideas that aren't our own, even when we are not quoting or paraphrasing. For example:

> The National Auto Safety Administration says teenage drivers react faster than older drivers.

Ideas that are well known and generally accepted don't need attribution. For example, it wouldn't be necessary to attribute the statement, "Alcohol can slow a driver's reactions."

If there's any doubt about whether an idea should be attributed or not, it's a good idea to ask the person who assigned the research.

Charts, Graphs, and Statistics

Let's say that a student finds a big chart giving all kinds of statistics on driver reaction times on the Web site of the National Auto Safety Administration. The student wants to use the chart in his or her paper, but only wants to include the relevant information. He or she might take out the necessary information and present it like this:

Driver age	Average driver reaction time
16	0.5 seconds
50	1.5 seconds

Source: National Auto Safety Administration

If the figures are included as a sentence in the paper's written text, the information still needs to be attributed:

The average reaction time for sixteen-year-old drivers is one-half second, compared with 1.5 seconds for fifty-year-olds, according to the National Auto Safety Administration.

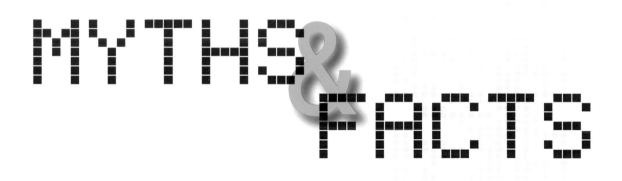

MYTHS & FACTS

MYTH Wikipedia is a good research source.

FACT Wikipedia and other "Wiki" sites aren't accepted sources for most research. Anyone can contribute to a Wikipedia entry, regardless of his or her qualifications. It's difficult and often impossible to determine who the contributors are. There are plenty of facts on Wikipedia, but there's also biased and inaccurate information. It isn't always possible to separate the facts from the bad information. However, Wikipedia can be useful. The "Notes," "References," and "External Links" sections at the bottom of Wikipedia articles can be helpful in tracking down information from solid sources.

MYTH I can find anything I need with Google.

FACT Google is a great starting point for most research. But finding "anything" can be a problem. It's easy to get too much information. Initial searches can return so much irrelevant material that it can be hard to tell where to begin. Searches need to be refined, then refined again to narrow down the results. Sometimes it's actually faster and easier to use a reference book. Asking a librarian might be the best move of all—when it comes to asking questions and getting explanations, there's no substitute for talking to a real person.

MYTH I can find anything I need on the Internet.

FACT Not always. The best place to look for sources depends on the research topic. Many Internet sources aren't available to everyone. Some sites or parts of sites are password protected; users need to belong to a group or organization. Sometimes users have to pay for information. We might be able to find a list of books on our topic, but then we have to buy the book we need. Much of the best research is the kind that we do ourselves by interviewing sources in person or on the phone or by corresponding with them.

Chapter 5

Detective Work

Professional investigators save time and effort by knowing the best places to search for clues. A researcher can find quick clues about the credibility of his or her sources by looking closely at certain parts of our media.

A Closer Look at Web Sites

The URL, or uniform resource locator, is the line of letters and numbers that usually begins with http:// in the browser's address space. URLs can reveal several things about the page on the screen.

Top-level domain (TLD) designations are three-letter codes. The most familiar is probably ".com." TLDs often indicate what kind of organization is hosting the page.

Colleges and universities use ".edu." These can have plenty of good sources, but beware! Some ".edu" sites host joke pages.

Governments in the United States use ".gov" and can be good sources of official information.

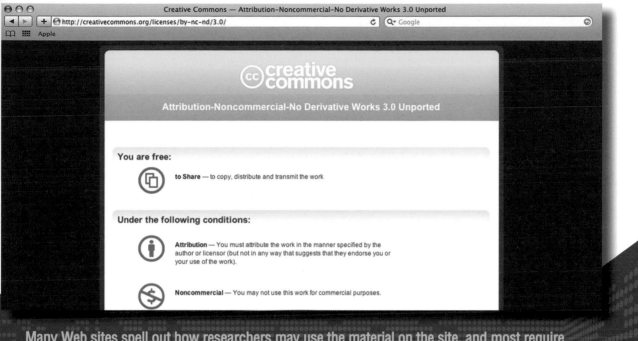

Many Web sites spell out how researchers may use the material on the site, and most require attribution. Creative Commons (http://creativecommons.org) is a nonprofit organization that helps people grant different kinds of copyright permissions to their work.

Several years ago, ".com" was set aside for commercial businesses, ".org" for nonprofit and charity groups, and ".net" for Internet service providers. Now just about anyone can use one of these designations.

Personal pages are often indicated by a tilde (~) or a percent sign (%), followed by a person's name. Also, look for words in the URL like "host," "users," or "members," which indicate someone's personal Web page on a commercial host such as AOL. Before using material from a personal page, remember the two-part test for credibility.

The letters right after http:// or http://www in most URLs are the name of the server. The server designation often indicates the organization that's putting the information on the Internet. For example, a URL that begins with "http://www.nytimes.com" shows that the page was published by the *New York Times*.

File   Edit   View   Favorites   Tools   Help

WHAT DOES THE ORGANIZATION SAY ABOUT ITSELF?

What Does the Organization Say About Itself?

Source organizations usually say something about themselves on their Web sites. Look for links at the top, bottom, or edges of the page that say things like "About Us," "Information," or "Mission Statement."

Most sites have a "Contacts" link that lists officers in the organization and says how to get more information. Most sites include information that indicates when the page was last updated. It is often found at the bottom of the page. Some sites post "Conditions for Use" of their material. Read before using! For student use, educational sites usually ask only that they be credited.

Web sites that specialize in information about other sites can be handy evaluation tools. They show who owns a site, what kind of information it handles, and how much traffic it has. They may also say how many other sites link to it and how users rate its quality. Sites like Alexa.com and AboutUs.org. provide free searches and information about other sites.

Blogs, Books, and Printed Articles

Credible blogs always identify the sources of their information, and posting dates should be easy to find. Many bloggers also post links to their biographies so that readers can judge their qualifications. Sometimes it may be necessary to do a search on an individual blogger's name to find his or her qualifications. If no sources, posting dates, or qualifications are given anywhere, it's probably time to find another source.

Books usually have their printing dates on one of the very first pages. Author information is usually on the book jacket or cover or on one of the pages just before or after the main text.

Web searches can turn up a lot of information—sometimes too much to handle. Asking for help from a librarian is often a time-saver.

Most newspapers and magazines put the date of their publication on the front page or cover. Look for writers' names at the top or bottom of each article. If the writer works for the publication, there may not be a separate biography. Most publications have staff information on their Web sites.

Librarians can usually tell us a lot about source publications. For online information, search "newspaper directories" or "magazine directories."

Logic and Argument

We've looked at ways to check the reliability of our sources. We've discussed ways to check material for accuracy and relevance. We've examined how

Argument can mean trying to persuade someone that an idea is correct. In logic, it also means a set of statements that lead to a conclusion. Debaters use both kinds of argument.

to use facts fairly. Now let's ask a final big question about the information we've found: Does it make sense?

Logic is a huge area of study that figures into just about every subject. Researchers use logic to evaluate source information and present their own information in ways that make sense.

Logic focuses on the ways that we draw conclusions, mostly from statements that we accept for the purpose of argument. In logic, argument doesn't mean disagreement. A logical argument is a step-by-step way of reaching a conclusion. Arguments usually consist of several statements followed by a conclusion. There are two basic types of argument: deductive and inductive.

Deductive arguments often start with a general statement, followed by more specific statements. In a deductive argument, if all the statements are facts, the conclusion must be a fact. For example:

All cats are mammals. (Fact)
My pet Snowball is a cat. (Fact)
Therefore, Snowball is a mammal. (Must be a fact)

Inductive arguments usually start with a statement about a specific thing, followed by broader statements. In inductive arguments, statements are used to support a conclusion that's probably a fact. For example:

Snowball is a cat.
Most cats like to lie in the sun.
Therefore, Snowball probably likes to lie in the sun.

The conclusions of our arguments can be used as the beginning statements for new arguments. That's a major way that research advances knowledge. Facts lead to new facts.

Arguments can also result in false conclusions, even when all the statements are true. For example:

All cats are mammals. (Fact)
My pet Snowball is a mammal. (Fact)
Therefore, Snowball is a cat. (Not necessarily a fact)

Does that argument prove Snowball is a cat? No. She might be a dog, a hamster, or any other type of mammal. That kind of mistaken argument is called a fallacy. There are many types of fallacies. Some sources use the language of logic—words like "therefore" and "so"—to make their information sound like proven fact. Don't be fooled. Look for a real argument. Statements that sound logical may be nothing more than biased opinion.

TEN GREAT QUESTIONS
TO ASK A LIBRARIAN

1. What's a reliable place to find sources of information about my research topic?

2. Who or what is the best primary source for that information?

3. What's the source's purpose in publishing the information?

4. Does the source have a special point of view?

5. Where can I find out what others think about that source?

6. Where can I find other points of view about the information?

7. How old is the information?

8. What are the best secondary sources for the information about my subject?

9. Do any of the sources have reason to be biased?

10. Is there any reason why this information shouldn't be used in my research paper?

GLOSSARY

argument In logic, a series of statements leading to a conclusion.

attribution Identification of a source of information.

bias The way a source's point of view affects the way that information is presented. Sources aren't always conscious of their bias.

conclusion The result of a logical argument, or the outcome of research.

credibility Believability. Credible sources are ones that we can trust.

disinformation Material that isn't true and is known by the source to be untrue.

fact True information. Facts can be tested and verified.

fallacy A mistaken logical argument.

format Repetition in the way that information is presented in order to make the information seem familiar and credible.

information What sources say or show; words, pictures, data, and other material that we can examine to find facts.

innuendo Leaving out facts but implying a conclusion; letting readers or viewers draw conclusions from things that aren't stated.

misinformation Information that isn't true, although the source believes it is.

opinion An idea that someone thinks or believes; a statement that can't be proved true or false.

plagiarism Using a source's words or ideas without giving credit to the source; the theft of words or ideas.

propaganda Biased information that's intended to persuade readers, listeners, or viewers to do certain things or think in certain ways.

publish To make information public.

sensationalism A form of hyperbole that often distorts facts.

source An origin of information. Sources are usually people, groups of people, or artifacts.

FOR MORE INFORMATION

Canadian Journalism Project
117 Peter Street, 3rd Floor
Toronto, ON M5V 2G9
Canada
(416) 955-0630
Web site: http://www.j-source.ca
The Canadian Journalism Project of the Canadian Journalism Foundation pro-
    motes excellence in journalism, information, and commentary. Its site has
    news, research, advice, discussion, and other resources, including tools for
    locating sources, tools for ensuring accuracy, and tools for Web research.

Library of Congress
101 Independence Avenue SE
Washington, DC 20540
(202) 707-5000
Web site: http://www.loc.gov/families
The Library of Congress is the research arm of the U.S. Congress and has
    the largest library in the world. It offers programs and online resources
    for students, including "Ask a Librarian," Webcasts with famous people,
    and sections on history, music, and many other subjects.

Media Awareness Network
1500 Merivale Road, 3rd Floor
Ottawa, ON K2E 6Z5
Canada
(613) 224-7721
Web site: http://www.media-awareness.ca
The Media Awareness Network promotes critical thinking about the media. It
    produces programs and resources for teachers, parents, and students.

Smithsonian Institution
Center for Education and Museum Studies
P.O. Box 37012, MRC 508
Washington, DC 20013-7012
(202) 633-5330
Web site: http://www.si.edu
The Smithsonian Institution is the world's largest museum complex and
research organization. It sponsors a variety of education programs. Its
online encyclopedia has information about arts and design, history and
culture, and science and technology.

Young Adult Library Services Association
50 East Huron Street
Chicago, IL 60611
(800) 545-2433, ext. 4390
Web site: http://www.ala.org
The Young Adult Library Services Association promotes library service for
students aged twelve to eighteen. It sponsors Teen Read Week and
Teen Tech Week. It has a Teen Top Ten favorite book list and other
online book lists for research.

Web Sites

Due to the changing nature of Internet links, Rosen Publishing has developed
an online list of Web sites related to the subject of this book. This site is
updated regularly. Please use this link to access the list:

http://www.rosenlinks.com/dil/cited

FOR FURTHER READING

Arnone, Marilyn P., Sharon Coatney, and Gerry Stockley. *The Curious Kids . . . Digging for Answers: A Storybook Approach to Introducing Research Skills* (Mac, Information Detective). Santa Barbara, CA: Greenwood Publishing Group, 2006.

Badke, William. *Research Strategies: Finding Your Way Through the Information Fog*. Lincoln, NE: iUniverse, 2008.

Cooper, Sheila, and Rosemary Patton. *Writing Logically, Thinking Critically*. 6th ed. New York, NY: Longman Publishing Group, 2009.

Dublin, Anne. *June Callwood: A Life in Action*. Victoria, BC, Canada: Orca Book Publishers, 2007.

Editors of *Time for Kids* Magazine. *Time for Kids Almanac 2010*. New York, NY: Time, Inc., Home Entertainment, 2009.

George, Mary W. *The Elements of Library Research; What Every Student Needs to Know*. Princeton, NJ: Princeton University Press, 2008.

Goodwin, Susan W., and Peggy J. Whitley. *99 Jumpstarts for Kids' Social Studies Reports: Research Help for Grades 3–8*. Santa Barbara, CA: Greenwood Publishing, 2007.

Jakubiak, David J. *A Smart Kid's Guide to Doing Internet Research*. New York, NY: Rosen Publishing Group, 2009.

Lenburg, Jeff. *The Facts on File Guide to Research*. New York, NY: Checkmark Books, 2005.

Lester, James D. *Writing Research Papers: A Complete Guide*. 13th ed. New York, NY: Longman Publishing Group, 2009.

McGuigan, Brendan, Douglas Grudzina, and Paul Moliken. *Rhetorical Devices: A Handbook and Activities for Student Writers*. Clayton, DE: Prestwick House, 2007.

O'Donnel, Liam. *Media Meltdown: A Graphic Guide Adventure*. Victoria, BC, Canada: Orca Book Publishers, 2009.

Orr, Tamra. *Extraordinary Research Projects*. London, England: Franklin Watts, 2008.

Polette, Nancy. *Stop the Copying with Wild and Wacky Research Projects*. Westport, CT: Libraries Unlimited, 2008.

Ruschmann, Paul. *Media Bias: Point Counterpoint*. Philadelphia, PA: Chelsea House, 2006.

Skog, Jason. *Yellow Journalism*. Mankato, MN: Capstone Press. 2007.

Sniderman, Alex. *Plato: The Father of Logic*. New York, NY: Rosen Publishing Group, 2006.

Somervill, Barbara A. *What Are the Facts? Collecting Information*. New York, NY: Rosen Publishing Group, 2007.

Veit, Richard. *Research: The Student's Guide to Writing Research Papers*. 4th ed. Needham Heights, MA: Allyn & Bacon, 2003.

Warlick, David. *Classroom Blogging*. 2nd ed. Morrisville, NC: Lulu.com, 2007.

Weston, Anthony. *A Rulebook for Arguments*. 4th ed. Indianapolis, IN: Hackett Publishing, 2009.

BIBLIOGRAPHY

Arrington, Michael. "Facebook Now Nearly Twice the Size of MySpace Worldwide." TechCrunch.com, January 22, 2009. Retrieved September 17, 2009 (http://www.techcrunch.com/2009/01/22/facebook-now-nearly-twice-the-size-of-myspace-worldwide).

Cornell University Library. "How to Evaluate the Information Sources You Find." February 29, 2008. Retrieved September 15, 2009 (http://www.library.cornell.edu/olinuris/ref/research/evaluate.html).

Henderson, John. "ICYouSee: T Is for Thinking." Ithaca College, August 26, 2009. Retrieved September 2, 2009 (http://www.ithaca.edu/library/training/think.html).

Kies, Daniel. "Using Logic in Composition." Department of English, College of DuPage, December 27, 2008. Retrieved September 22, 2009 (http://papyr.com/hypertextbooks/comp1/logic.htm).

Purdue Owl. "Avoiding Plagiarism: Safe Practices." September 30, 2008. Retrieved October 1, 2009 (http://owl.english.purdue.edu/owl/resource/589/03).

Rozakis, Laurie. *Shaum's Quick Guide to Writing Great Research Papers*. New York, NY: McGraw-Hill, 1999.

Smith, Alastair. *The Usborne Guide to Homework on the Internet*. London, England: Usborne Publishing, 2002.

Turabian, Kate L. *A Manual for Writers of Research Papers, Theses, and Dissertations*, 7th ed. Chicago, IL: University of Chicago Press, 2007.

UC Berkeley. "Evaluating Web Pages: Techniques to Apply and Questions to Ask." Teaching Library Internet Workshops, August 11, 2009. Retrieved September 15, 2009 (http://www.lib.berkeley.edu/TeachingLib/Guides/Internet/Evaluate.html).

U.S. Department of Justice. "Crime and Victims Statistics." Bureau of Justice Statistics, August 2008. Retrieved September 17, 2009 (http://ojp.usdoj.gov/bjs/cvict.htm).

INDEX

A

AboutUs.org, 36
Alexa.com, 36
attribution, 19, 29, 30–32

B

bias, 10–12, 14, 16, 17, 39
blogs/bloggers, 10, 16, 36

C

citizen journalists, 10
commercial media, 21–22

D

deductive arguments, 38, 39
disinformation, 13, 17–19

E

emotional/inflammatory language, 19
exaggeration, 19

G

gossip, 19

I

ideas, attributing, 31
inductive arguments, 38, 39
innuendo, 19

J

jargon, 23

M

media, definition of, 6–7
misinformation, 13, 17

O

opinion disguised as fact, 13–14

P

paraphrases, attributing, 30–31
plagiarism, 27–30
primary sources, 8–9
propaganda, 13, 14–18

Q

quotations, attributing, 30

R

rumor, 19

S

secondary sources, 8, 9–10
sensationalism, 22, 23
social media, 10
sources, definition of, 6–7
statistics, attributing, 31–32

T

top-level domain (TLD) designations, 34–35
Twitter, 10

U

URLs, 34–35

About the Author

Larry Gerber has been doing research in person, in libraries, and on the Internet for more than thirty-five years. He has edited newspapers and magazines, and he is a former Associated Press foreign correspondent and bureau chief. Gerber lives in Los Angeles, where he now does independent writing and editing.

Photo Credits